A New Flora:

Sapphic Poems from the Garden of Lesbos

by

Jessica Lowell Mason

Finishing Line Press
Georgetown, Kentucky

A New Flora:

Sapphic Poems from the Garden of Lesbos

For *Sappho*,
for the moon,
for the flower
when she blooms.

*In memory of the gardener who made my favorite gardener
Nicola Cieri (1919 - 2002)*

Copyright © 2025 by Jessica Lowell Mason
ISBN 979-8-89990-064-8 First Edition
All rights reserved under International and Pan-American Copyright Conventions. No part of this book may be reproduced in any manner whatsoever without written permission from the publisher, except in the case of brief quotations embodied in critical articles and reviews.

ACKNOWLEDGMENTS

With great thanks to those who are part of the fellowship of artists and writers that has helped to form and encourage the flow of language in me, especially Chris Iwanicki, Sackville West, Lawrence Rowswell, Viv, Kathleen Bryce Niles, and the writers of the Herstory workshop, "Memoirs to (Re)Imagine Mental Healthcare (2021 - 2025). With tender thanks to the gardeners who have inspired me to nurture love, especially Ro Cieri and our garden's most precious treasures, our lily and our rose.

Publisher: Leah Huete de Maines
Editor: Christen Kincaid
Cover Art: Abhipsa Chakraborty
Author Photo: Jessica Lowell Mason
Cover Design: Elizabeth Maines McCleavy

Order online: www.finishinglinepress.com
also available on amazon.com

Author inquiries and mail orders:
Finishing Line Press
PO Box 1626
Georgetown, Kentucky 40324
USA

Contents

At Garden Gates	1
The Essential Objects of Deadly Days	2
Between the Innkeeper and the Inn	4
Into Furious Being	6
A Path None can Abandon	7
Grief is the Seed	8
Submerged	9
Decade of the Grave	10
The Future is Funereal	12
We are a Psychedelic Relic	14
Flora Fire	15
The Garden They Fear	16
Anon Entity	17
Guarden Friend	18
An Invitation	19
The Root and Room of Three	20
A Gradual Resistance	22
The Thought of Being	23
A Canvas Speaking King	24
Smash the Glass, Claim the Hours	25
Hospitality of the Mind	26
Come the Cape and the Woman	27
Voodoo Doll Planet	28
Second Story	29
Milk and Honey and Hex	30
The Tree Must First Survive	32
Between Us is a Galaxy	34
Dr. Frankenstein's Defense	36
An Act of Death	38
In Defiance of Cruel Fate	40
OB S(e)curity and Our Necessary Vulgarities	41

I am molten lava erupting into you	43
To Raise Monsters	44
Today, A Flock of Orchids	45
I Ask the Lilacs	47
Coconut Woman	48
The Angry Daffodils	50
Ferns and Fears	51
A New Flora	53
Dear Vita, Don't Delay	54
Truth Stated Plainly is in Danger	55
Under a Sixfold Sun	56
Roots	57
Hanami on the First Day of Spring (A Schoolyard Liturgy for the Winter-Buried)	58
And Now I Live for the Flowers	60
How Grief and I Relate	62
In This Reality, Rare	63
From Sky to You	64
Pansy Lips	65
You Pair Well with Me	66
The Well of Lo	67
You, Becoming a Flower in Bloom	68
My Petals Weep	69
Perenal	70
What's a Sunflower	71
These Words, My Vespers	72
Is Grief a Demon or a Daffodil?	73

"Last night, at sunset,
The foxgloves were like tall altar candles.
Could I have lifted you to the roof of the greenhouse,
my Dear,
I should have understood their burning."

Amy Lowell, "Vespers" from *What's O'Clock*

At Garden Gates

We go to the womb
to look for a beginning

but the womb
evaporates into an ether;

we go to injustice,
to look for justice

but these roads
are such long roads,

and we will meet the dirt
before we become

the light; we claw
and crawl across

unspoken terrains,
coffin kids, playing

games with death,
we go to gardens

in our heads,
towers in our cities,

to look for answers,
but bodies leap

from ten story windows,
and we come crashing

down; we go to rows
of tulips to find our names

but we are stopped
at garden gates.

The Essential Objects of Deadly Days

We are now living on dumpster time.
Dumpster time is told in threes and by the nose,
a waltz up a shaft of banana peels: oh, how time slides.

The garbage trucks are the latest watches,
they take the anality of the masses out of our sight
and deliver it to the side of town where cancer grows.

Three times a week, there is a crashing sound,
and this is how we know there has been division, music,
that we are part of a third of something, but what?

Three metal bangs and three stories of three buildings
of residents who know something has been collected,
and that it is either a Monday, a Wednesday—or a Friday.

When the siss boom bang of garbage ceases,
that is how the trash-kept know the time has come
to take out white stretched bags of liquids and hair balls.

Our drains are clogged, our toilets, rammed with feces,
our tiles are crumbling, but we wash in thirds:
we are, if not clean, then whatever is next to that.

We start to notice that the mountain is higher than
the container, we do the math: three buildings are not full,
there are vacancies, this garbage is coming in from an outside.

We start to notice that the refuse from poverty and hoarding,
that strange combination, is gathering in a spectacle here
in this parking lot. We are its beholders, beholden.

Each of us has room with a view of bed-bug infested
couches and mattresses, martyrs and their springs, mixed
with the sludge of the sump pumps from all over town.

We are a hot commodity; our neighbors value us;
they send their shit and diseases here; we are needed;
they have nowhere else to go; these are the front lines.

We are living in the age of certain death,
we are living where the excesses of waste gather,
this dumpster is a metaphor packed too full.

We are making something—it is not nice,
the line between dumpster and landfill has been crossed
and the travel time between the two ever diminishes.

This city is teaming with trash. Is it ours or is it us?
Is this what we will call planet, what we will call planetary
or are we and our overflow a universe's curse?

We are unable to give in to deep sighs, in this pile
of thrown-away life, I read the expression of objects,
the shape of violence, how it forms a deadly bouquet.

Between the Innkeeper and the Weed

You cannot kill a weed.
The doctor tried three times
and it didn't work.

A salty innkeeper shares
her garden wisdom, its acerbic
bed of indestructible herbs.

What does it take, now, to be a weed,
to root into life with a vengeance?
What is the new immortal?

Is one born a weed
or is a weed something one can become,
a life-affirming claimed identity?

A weed climbs the stairs,
lays the limbs of her grain against
the grains of the wood.

The weed that keeps the inn,
she holds the crease between
her stems, where there is pain.

She indicates in gestures
what must be the trauma
suffered by weeds in order to live.

But then she thanks the doctor
she once likened to a weed-killer,
and occupies space in the contradiction.

Her body speaks over her,
she gestures to a wound
hidden under her garments.

She teaches me to learn the signs
of weeds, to laugh when weeds speak,
to feel something being kept beneath.

The weed is not the immortal
she claims to be, but there is a prayer
between the innkeeper and the weed.

Into Furious Being

A few of us

      (the flaming saints)

are lucky:

      we give birth to dragons.

We defy the rules

      of the womb

and lay raging eggs.

      A few of us do.

And even fewer

      give birth to dragons

      in the womb.

We fire up our loins,

      coax our cauldrons,

and bubble baby dragons

      (the babes of flames)

into furious being.

A Path None can Abandon

A somber garden awaits us—

she is streaked with muted pain,

the moon above her is a captive,

we see her shadow-swallowed light,

we are the trees trimmed to nothing,

we are the timber tumbling, thudding,

along a path none can abandon

where all the sun's wishes die,

and each day is the last day.

A somber garden awaits us—

in her plots are rows of corpses,

we wonder, from us, what will grow:

she is the destiny of flies and worms,

and we are part of this dismal burial,

we tilled this land to death

and we are its interior design;

now the air has a price on its head,

now we are the somber garden,

but the gardener is dead.

Grief is the Seed

My child, you were given grief
as a seed to grow a garden
of empathy, where the serpents
are not of the apples but pierce
as the edges of pitchforks
in hands that tear rather than till.

Your soil you must soak
in others' tears, your roots
will be painfully formed,
as each tendril that multiplies
and spreads itself in the name
of keeping you grounded
will depend on a watershed.

Love the grief that soaks
your spirit and spreads your
beginnings. You cannot flee the fork
or its tear but if the underground
you've made is vast enough,
some part of you always survives.

Submerged

During the death years,
when death was heavy within us,

when we were paddling
and panting in lakes of death,

when we were up to our necks,
I devoted my head to thoughts of you.

Decade of the Grave

I hope we have broken through
something here, reaching our arms

out of the graves,

this was the new decade,
taken   away,

there are words that cannot
be used

to describe this,
yet we will have to dig

into our plots
            to find   a way

to say what the clock
of moons refuses

in her stoic contemplation,
where illusions go to dissolve,

where our shipments are delayed
but still on their way;

we wait—will Capitalism
deliver

not on time, but *in time*,
yet we know the answer,

the ground up earth
in our mouths,

the dust we are becoming
first appears within us

and as hearts race in the night,
with the pounding of the undone,

we wade in our places of unrest
across a riverbed of unknowns.

The Future is Funereal

We do not know the gravediggers
that are to come,

we do not know the shovels
we'll soon hold, the ways

our backs will hunch,
the rows and rows of the newly

employed lowering the bodies,
the lumber stocks that will rise

when the demand for caskets
skyrockets, the size of the load

of dirt it will take to cover
what must be hidden from the mind,

the surplus of cemetery jobs,
the price of deadland,

the micro-homes of ash
and bones; we do not know

the funereal age, what new botany
and how much incense we will need

to cover the stench of these days,
the way we will gather, side by side,

the way we will fill the plots,
the way we will come in droves,

the way our economy
will boom,

the culture of grieving,
the chorus of secluded sighs,

the daily goodbyes, the (repetitive)
ends, the troubles ahead.

We are a Psychedelic Relic

The portal of Language,
and her potentialities,
evokes an art
of disappearance,
there are liquid platforms,
the melting of our thoughts,
the catapult into yearning,
the bubbling nova
of discerning,
that can take us in, too,
to reach a place unreached,
released in her infinity,
the more we know of her,
the more we disappear,
we are the voices we hear,
we are queer, but here,
knowing is a moment,
an entry and a deconstruction
of participles in every
direction, including
the inward participle,
the play within
foreplay enters our
conjoined minds,
opens our mouths,
and her tongue moves
in us, between us,
she is the talisman,
we are the epiphany,
we are her quakes,
the planet shatters
while we exchange
her glorious brokenness;
we will never remember
the contents, but
to the experience
our wonder is bound.

Flora Fire

The violins of midnight
flow along the quivering
planes of time-hidden
light; there is no moon
here now, but we still have
what can't be seen by sight;
there is a rising of strange
horizons beneath these
burning beds: our library
of desire, our dreaming
flora fire, blue-red.

The Garden They Fear

Not a stain on the sole
of the shoe, he notes,

as we grope space and time
for a trace of a soul.

I gather the fragments
and make a bouquet.

It can't be delivered,
but it can be displayed.

We hold the arrangement,
we hold the formation,

we know its paper logic,
we know its disarray:

a truth dispersed
that will never cohere

for those who are prone
to puzzle and sneer;

I scatter the bouquet,
there's the garden they fear.

Anon Entity

I was Joan and Jane
and you were Jane and Joan.

I am a tender wild with a
wild tender will to give
my bones, my lives, my cries
my armor

to

anon entity—

when you went down,
deflated the outer self
enough, when it all turned
gelatinous, when you were
no longer tethered to a form,
when you were a voice
in the safe space
of a free mind:

that was when I felt you:
sensed, understood, knew.

Guarden Friend

And where has my gracious friend gone?
The way of the sky, deep into the dirt?
I cannot find her here on Earth.

And so I hold my friend aloft;
I keep her trust, I keep her in the soft
(est) regions of my thoughts.

I keep my friend where I know her
best, know her dry, know her wet;
I keep her knit within my breast.

I keep her sweet and sour and safe,
I hold her bitterly, bold, like fate;
my friend is held in my embrace.

Beneath an armor kingdoms high,
across my chest, between my thighs,
the guardian of all my sighs.

She is what keeps me chained and free,
when I ward off women, when I ward off men,
I am left alone, at peace, with my friend.

But when I think of signs and meaning,
I think of my friend and begin bleeding
palms and psalms, and devotional readings.

Just when I fear the woods she keeps,
with sword and shield, I go in deep;
my friend is lost in a maze of deceit.

So where has my gracious friend gone?
The way of the dark, the way of the dust;
I look to the woods and choose to trust:

My gracious friend, my sacred self,
when sorrows rise and faith rewinds
my ancient guardian abides.

An Invitation

Come down and be,
with the mother on her knees

if she drools, hold the towel,
cradle it in your hands,
pull it taut, wait,

and if you can give her
her baby, do, and if you cannot
give her   her baby

do not refuse to gather her
tears in a basin

dark and bleak

if the mother on her knees
guts you, enters her moans
into the space in you she carved
out for her grief,

then be with her: drool, weep.

The Root and Room of Three

For love, life, grief,
and the root of three,
mirror into mirror
into mirror, and in them
all I see: their eyes
in my eyes, one jolted
awake, one laughing,
one with rivers
because perfect love
always flows,
sometimes violently,
and I am a river
rapid now, opened
as wide as when my mind
sensed your eyes
open, a wise half-soul
waiting for whole
to find love itself gazing
in stillness lighting
up the cave in me,
I shift between them
grief—grief—grief
for loving is so great
that when bereft
it debilitates and repeats
to live, to be in,
to feel one with sand, sod,
to feel,
to push one's toes
through wall after wall
after wall, to damage
one's hands, to flutter
briefly into webs
of faced fears, to smash
time with love and then
to feel one's feet
at the center,
on a teeter-totter,

balancing all inwardly,
this grief so great
because this love: is,
and there is enough,
enough room,
to feel the knives
of false grass, the blades
of man, and still
to stand, enough
room in me to love
what cannot help
but pull our little lives
into the slats
of muck as I reach
into the air
for love, for life, for grief.

A Gradual Resistance

The stillness of the tree is forbidden
in these times, when stillness is an invitation
to debauchery; she might catch fire,
she might catch ice, she might blow,
her roots might give, she might end
up breaking the house built
of a less-formidable substance than her
trunk and limbs, she stands tall,
a soothing ominous victim waiting to be
wrecked and then blamed, her silence
admirable, her silence infuriating,
her silence unreadable, her silence not
silence, her voice unconquerable, she speaks
in a language the bulldozer cannot
comprehend, but it plow and hearths
her anyway, she will not come to life,
but she has been alive, all this time
has crept into life in a gradual
resistance, and I will creep into her roots,
and into her sister's roots, sacrifice
my decay to her when I leave man-(un)kind
to become one with what soaks into her,
when he releases us from captivity,
when I am claimed and belong to what he
has forbid, the air a tiny girl will breathe,
when I am the forbidden stillness deep
within (when I am) the tree that lives.

The Thought of Being

Through windows, fragments of trees
cut down aloft by the bifurcation of sight,
I curse in anguish at the vanquished moon,
I am the beast that longs for you,

these chalkboards without chalk haunt
the hollow planks, one cry from one coyote
would send me into a terror, one apparition
of the compact that reflects all metaphors,

one reminder of love suspended, of constancy
aloft and soft, would lull me into sweet
docility, but night gnaws on, shredding
mercies inside of these inner chambers

that hellish twilights uncover in me,
I am becoming Nefertiti, a paralysis
and an ancient awareness of a self

that cannot be reconstructed and will be
reductive, that will condemn me
to a chaste coffin of agony, but somehow
the thought of being an artifact, a fact

of complexity reduced to the fragments
of myth, somehow to be returned to symbols
and signs is a fitting punishment
for the crime of thought, I will deconstruct

the monster until the maiden will arise,
I am the symbols and signs that long
to be disassembled and resurrected
through these windows, fragments of these.

A Canvas Speaking King

The papier-mâché cloud of memory
hovers over you and you sit at your desk,
the faces of moments behind you,
where are you now and what do you
forget, and are you aware that I am
a canvas speaking to you,
there are no words in this, my eyes tell
you to throw away technique, to forget
that you cannot remember, to be here
without fear, to stroke boldly, with failure,
to scribble into oblivion,
to strike out self-consciousness
from your consciousness, unloose
the animal from the narrative,
or do you live in a gilded world
where even a toilet can be made
of gold, will mud and meaninglessness
not do, but I cry tears of golden vapor
for you, and I collect apples in my
likeness and make myself a shriveled
head for you, and I say flounder in what the mist
sets down until you float, until the cage
bars form a moat, a soaking crossroads
into something new, until pencils grow
from your hands, this is the safety
of failure, beckoning you, what is left
when you are alone in the ecstasy
of forgetting, when the eyes on the canvas
and the artist recede, when the eyes
inside emerge from the gallows
of conjecture, judgment, and triviality.

Smash the Glass, Claim the Hours

Stopped at the peak of infinity,
we graduated into an hour glass,
were told to turn back

from life.

I lie in the plot beside your grave,
and remind you of all I gave,

to life.

I ask the earth, the binding earth,
to be the flower I was becoming

to ascend into the star I became

when I ascended into life,

but I am (with the) gravel, remembering
the stillness of the astonished moon

when I gave you a broken clock,
a clock broken

with life, when you were
broken open by it,

before you buried
in your cave of bones

what was

(timeless).

Hospitality of the Mind

What are unwanted thoughts?

There was never a thought
that I didn't want, an atom
of life I did not embrace.
I relish the sign and code.

If thoughts are guests,
this inn is open,
this inn will never close.

What are unwanted guests?

The guests here are all born
of the desire of the innkeeper,
and my guest of honor is you
in a thousand disguises.

I love when you enter moustached,
holding a petunia like a cigar,
and you smoke the stem.

I want you in the inn
of my thoughts,
where
you are always welcome.

Come the Cape and the Woman

Come the symbolic gestures,
come the incomprehensible hopes,
come the cape and the woman
it adorns, the one who sings with Cohen
but amends the lyrics, "I'm your batman."

Come the end of the to-dos and the end
of all the don'ts, come the ghosts
back from the dead to haunt the liars
in their beds until they all confess,
come lay your head upon my breast,
until your skull cuts through my chest.

Come your lust for my treasures, come
my most chaste treasures to your lips,
come the old goodness to fight back
the wreck, come the shackles in your head
that keep you from a better path.

Come your saintliness, and in its likeness,
your sins, come the past to play the herald
and the usher, come the writing desk
and its wings, come the swings without
the middle-aged whiplash, come the flagrant
closets, unloosing liberation and its fragrance.

Come the early modern heretical sages
and their reduced, conflated lives,
come all the unhappy wives to the streets,
to the boats, sailing off to make their oaths
to Paradise, come the armor to cover the girls
in their beds visited by terrors in the night.

Come the books to the hands of the children,
come the shields and the wings and the zaps
of laser beams, come the soft bedrock and the strong
streams, come the women floating up rivers,
come the ignored histories, on repeat.

Voodoo Doll Planet

If we are honest then we must admit that it is love
in the present tense, and that is always love,
and that we made the past so extraordinary
that it now makes us and will not yield
to rearview metaphors and primordial clichés,
this is a queer dimension, here is a queer telling
of time, from a dead pan planet that casts
its mute dread upon the drowning mop of earth
which names its rhymers, psychotics,
and its unreadable, autists, and that sinks
its Vicodin cocktail deeper and deeper
into its destiny, a wet collapse of farce
through the sieve of a dissolving illusion
in which addition and multiplication
lead to an infinity of division, civilization
dying for ages by diving into the deep end
of an arithmetic that could have no bottom
and no return route to oxygen, a thing of the past,
the sniveling earth is cruel and thrives on the agony
of simple subtractions, where soon the vegetative
will be without vegetation, and the consumer
will find itself commodified and consumed,
even the dead of the dead pan planet knows
it is love that breaks its own insistent metronomes,
here, now, without timing, I admit I give
to you myself as meteor, as debunked meteorology,
as burning balls and fire trails and silent canopies,
as desperate and sorrowful astrologies predicting
the past in order to claim the future, I am an arch inviting
you to walk away from this present subtraction, to crawl
into a futurity beyond algorithms, one that looks
like making the past that looks like making love,
like the past making love where the present is
wise and knows it is past and future colliding in the mouth
of an exasperated, cackling, groped consciousness
with buttons for eyes and pins in her planetary sides.

Second Story

Can you feel me, second story,
hanging precariously, above the world,
light and dry as pinched leaves, autumning,
heavy like a coconut in Paradise,
and just as ready
to crack,   to open   to you,
to witness mild surprise, milky elation,
the marvel of desire as it propels
desire, are you drenched now,
is your frock duly drenched, your under
garments forming to the mold of you,
are you reanimating, in your unseen finitude
of what is infinitely you, while you feel,
do you feel you pull
me to your mouth,
what it is to tip your head
back and then to hover
over what it is you love most,
human kindness, are you tuned
to the children's sermon
of our love that's filling pastoral mouths,
are you flickering the way our candles
flicker whether we light
them with our fingers or tongues,
are you with me, windows above,
second story   lives lived
in the arch of expressions,
in the rainbows, in the ungated bridges,
and the silent unidentified flying thunder,
can you feel the way we evaporate
into an inexplicable exponential?

Milk and Honey and Hex

To inhabit the conscience
is what we speak of

when we speak this beating,
flowing, flowering

metaphor,
the heart, the pumping vessel,

this
location unlocatable

except by us,

as air comes into you,
so do the particles

of the past,
and so do I,

sustaining tunnel,
the terror and trouble

of an unbreakable
pact, so tangled

up in you is my life
that each exhale you express

is expressed from
within me, milk and

honey and hex,
I bloom within your conscience

here, I am nine-month
ripened, the hag-faced

ancient child,
that which is to be:

mystic, mystifying fruit,
suspended in a womb,

concealed, concealing,
continuing,

connected to you
by the umbilical of the past,

in it the moments
we shared flow

and renew
from you to me to you.

The Tree Must First Survive

Tell me winter will not last,
or if it does, that it will end
with a kiss, with the mouth
of spring on its green nose
and neck, tell me that I will
arrive, that the dormant years
will have been worth the petals
that were forced to remain
an underground idea.

Today I am the tree, the merlot
maple, the seed covered in a belt
of rust, covered in a density
of stopped arrival, of a wetness
that cannot seep into growth,
with one rustle of my finger's
edge the whole could crack,
I am resigned to now, to making
each movement indecipherable,
to practicing microscopic agency.

When I had the will to write
myself across the seasons,
I recall what it felt like to stroke
a line of life that could not be
understood, I knew that was it,
what divinity felt like, eyes
peering up at you, and the split
between expressions, one caught
by the splendor of marvel
and another caught in the violent
throes of fear—that one lit
with pitchfork flames.

Some unearth with they cannot
worship, some throw their bodies
across what lay still to protect
what is gnarled with a meaning

out-of-reach, the sum of the first
some, the pitchforked, are those
to uproot salvation, to prolong
stagnation, but before we can talk
of flowers, the tree must first survive.

Between Us is a Galaxy

Meaning emanates
from the depths
of the soul,
and makes a garden
galaxy of the sea.

A man has sunk
his last, he is a ship
wrecked with hope
born of tumult,
and he sees in me
a beam.

I am a present past,
I am a garden sea,
I love a shipwrecked
ghost, and a ship
wrecked ghost
loves me.

Between us
is a sunken man,
between us
are the frozen trees,
between us
is a wreck of ages,
blue whispers
of eternity.

Light falls
from a wreckage
of stars,
and in us soar sparks
firmamentally.

I give you
my beam,
your host of the sea
I love you the most,
your mythos
is me.

Between us
is a standing wick,
between us
is the starry sea,
between us
is a subterrane,
a lilac flame,
a galaxy.

A constellation emanates
from the depths
of the sea,
and makes a garden
ghostship reef.

Dr. Frankenstein's Defense

The words you speak to me

multiply,

fracture, and multiply
again.

Your words have capacities
you do not

comprehend.

Like shadows, they grow,
becoming monsters

you will not control.

My mind is the mother
of these gargantuan beasts,

I'm in labor
as you cough out consonants,

each letter is a push,
each finished sentence,
a birth.

I nurture the offspring
of your ignorance,

I fatten them, love them,
release them

upon you and the world.

Your words are a runaway
experiment

over which a mother's heart,
a witch's art, will rule.

An Act of Death

She walks the grounds,
makes a labyrinth of the mundane,
finds meaning in the sorrow,
in the repetition; she wallows
endlessly, she shuffles fruitlessly,
she stops in front of the ice box,

she reaches in her gray hand,
there is no blood flow,
she cannot eat anything
that is not liquid, that was not
made with yeast, the popping
sounds of her existence, a can
opening, explodes in my head,

she makes light of her tragedy,
treads lightly through the maze,
I have come to be with her,
to join the gerbil in her cage,
I feel the weight of her ailments
sink into me and rise up
in many waves of frustration,

every tinge of rage in me
is a wish for whatever riches
would transport me
to the protest and leisure
of the active motherhood,
the act of motherhood,

which is no act but is the reason,
the reason stolen, my thoughts
escape the cage, leave
the grounds, soar and arrive
as halos, as crowns,

over the sweetest heads
of the smallest birds
with the strongest wings,
the spiritual sensation
that flew the cuckoo's
nest back into my womb.

In Defiance of Cruel Fate

Etched in the soul is a moment
of peace outstretched for eternity.

The sacred waning days
when as the hours slipped away

we were left with shattered clocks
and seconds suspended in space.

My two, my dears, sleep in peace
while I weep, wide awake

in the terrifying knowing
that a certain kind of gravity

defies and defines, and separates,
feel me reach for you

in defiance of cruel fate.

OB S(e)curity and Our Necessary Vulgarities

We know obscurity
too well, and we are
obscurity too often;
our lives, obscured,
our requests, obscured,
our demands, obscured,
our cries for help

o b   s   c   u   r   ed

but our bodies are still
desirable, still worth,
cramming, momentarily
claiming, still worth raping,
we feel the penetration
from across the room,
from across the screen,

we know they want
to fuck

our   brains   out

of us, we are at wit's end,
this is where we live,

wit's end,
it's a dead end but we plant
herbs there like green
zombies, we smudge
and smolder, we watch
the wreckage

go hissing up in smoke—

husbands, friends
of husbands,

husbands
of friends, stetho
scope-holders,
gavel-throwers,

strangers we haven't met,
at our doors again,
    waiting
at the edge of a dead
    end, calling
 the   last shreds
of   obscurity   out
of our hiding place,

they will fuck
even that,
    they will rape
      anything,
they will take everything,
including the ob

and the silent e
out of our
s   (e)   cur   it   y.

I am molten lava erupting into you.

To love freely, to let
the rays of the molten
globe of truth pour
and arch across
the coordinates of the world,
of flesh and thought,
is the only freedom
one can know, and it is
worth whatever it will be
called, however it will be
condemned
and misunderstood.

To Raise Monsters

My aim is not to raise daughters,
my aim is to raise monsters;
my aim is to be Hell and raise hellions,
out of the ash of my desire to be free
from having to fear for our safety,
my aim is to raise crazed fiends
who have the supernatural elements
to survive the maze of tombs that await
them, from my womb will come
the firebreathers who can char
to bits the fists and fist-held guns
of man into a pile of ash, molten-maidens,
half-child, half-bloodless hag,
harpies who give razorblade hairlip,
gorgons without guilt, offering nothing,
least of all explanations
for why it is, it will be, necessary to turn
to dust at an instant a vile memory
that the conscience is happy to forget,
serrated spirits and terrifying tellers
of alternative endings, where girls
stepping off busses grow bestial wings,
tiny targets no more, and animate gargoyles
detect intention, incinerating gazes,
rising up from wombs like hell,
with scales for armor, my aim is to raise
monsters who will never second guess
the decision to breathe fire and fly.

Today, A Flock of Orchids

We begin today with a flock of orchids,
in sublime morphology, we do not fear
the flying flowers, we begin today after
a night of sacred duress, of divestment
and of piecing together a hoard of crescents,
when we moved from room to room,
cradling the contents of a host of clueless
clues, wherein you leeched onto me
like spirited spores to a cellar flooded
with indiscriminate booze, when my swamped
chapters dissolved into your chest,
you pulled off my dust jackets, you drank
a tank of my ink, my words swirled into
you, rolled down your knees, you declared
me your library and favorite volume, you
consumed, read me, to the death,
on the shelves and under the covers,
and against the bookends, and in the dens,
and then on the study table, again,
I was eulogized through and through,
on the wobbly chair, citing prayers like friars
in our underwear, we were there, two
grooms at the table with Beethoven hair,
holding spoons, reciting satires in our diving
and divining attire, where we stood attuned
to the senses and spells of ruin, and we begin
today as flowers flying, spooning midair
in the roofless greenhouse, we greet today
awakened and awake to the closed collection
that has now been opened, librarians
and saints in a library only we can see,
we begin our day writhing our way
out of a surreptitious dream, we start
on a Julia Child favorite, covered in butter,
reveling in the joy of cooking up a scheme
to take down a crook in a crock pot deep
freeze, one thousand degrees of desires
below zero, we begin today with thunder,

with a recipe book, and chocolate rum
frosting, and one deep thrust, we concoct
too much, and it's not enough, we begin
today, a flock of orchids to the touch.

I Ask the Lilacs

In lilac sheets,
on lilac ice,
I make a bed
of lilac rice,
our tongues
they meet
in lilac time,
our words collide
in lilac rhymes,
I want you wet
with lilac dew,
I ask the lilacs:
is she true?

Coconut Woman

She lifts her head under the tree,
above she sees the ears of an ass,
the petals of a Hindi lily, the green
face of her love mocking the earth,
a heavenly minstrel, she thirsts
for psychotropic psychosis, a tropic
diagnosis, a theatre absurd: big nuts,
and of course unseen she thrusts
her thoughts like Seuss against
the trunk, she fancies herself neon
and a hunk, she hungers for the hard
knocks of coconuts, for the water,
the milk, and the creamy chaos,
she gives her mind to the humors
of windmill psalms, she's floored
and florid below the thrashing
flora of God, the mock-monarch
beside her grips his bong
but cannot light his tiki so he orders
a martini on the melting rocks,
what a sensible sky, what a perfect
day for ordinary lies, what a lovely
time to disregard the eminent tide,
to muse on retirement living, to be
lazy, unapologetic, and unforgiving,
to imagine a future of mausoleums,
to cruise through gated condominiums,
while she tans, while she scarfs,
while she chars, and clandestinely
scars, and strays with catgirls
with gin hair and fern skirts hiding
with limes and lemons, and screaming
cucumbers, behind skirted bars,
she takes swigs and laps in the purrs,
a life of palms and gin, until others
wonder: will the fruit fall far enough
from the tree to distract the cuck,

her thoughts come crashing, she's
a coconut that has aged long
and had enough, she's a woman
who craves a nutjob, who craves
her own nature from a beach of tar.

The Angry Daffodils

These are the angry daffodils,

they do not sing of spring,
they sting of hell, and you

have never heard of them,
unless you've strolled

out of poetics, into an angry

garden, where dissent
is the scent of the ascent

of an angry choir of hellion
daffodils; you'd never sense

botanic overwhelm unless you

were to travel there
with your floral death-wish,

making it past the riled
ramparts of raging

rhododendrons, over the hills

of had-enough hyacinths,
through the whiffs of furious

forget-me-nots and perturbed
petunias, into the haunted

woods of not-everything-is
-alliteration blue bells

who will not hold back
from telling you that

these daffodils are pissed.

Ferns and Fears

And when I was watering the ferns,
I was nurturing and feeding you,

those wrists that bent in hesitance,
those slow arcs of benevolence,

those flowering intentions, that watery
retention, those beads of attention,

those fingers frightened to overdo,
that spirit ever inclined to overflow,

the daily acts of a girl at a faucet
filling up a tin can, a girl who tilts

to keep alive the potted carceral soul
of wisdom unexpressed, the one

no longer known, but the greenest
fern envied you then, when we were

signs of the verdant times, now
buried under rubble and dumped

over with stones, a heaping myth
of feigned non-existence, housed

in vacant boxes of sealed resilience,
pods with transmutable seeds,

pockets of air where we are punctured
and doomed to containment,

where we are laden with the weight
of a forgotten age, where we seem

as gone as the days of greens
and grays when I gathered my tears

and watered, where all your years
were washed away, those steps you

took as you tiptoed through the gray
garden of caution, my first,

my only guardian, my nurtured,
my helper, when the ferns were fed

without the draught, without the dread,
without delay, where we were fed

fiddleheaded life at the window
of ferns and fears, where we traded

for greens our buckets of blues,
where now continue those hues anew,

where still nurtured is the life of the leaf,
the shrine of fronds and our living dead

A New Flora

You take the hard things down
into the deep of you and make
them your foundation, you build
roots firmly from the ruins
of beginnings that appeared
first as endings, you ground
yourself in a ground of yourself,
in a rich unbearable soil
of whatever broke you into you,
and you resolve to be the garden,
to be the garden's gardener,
to dig deep enough to be
a new flora, a sea-glass goddess
of power petals from beyond,
to bear absurd fruit, to be as soft
as you are sharp, as fiery
as you are buried in ice, to subdue
every serpent slithering near
into a living agent of change,
and you resolve to ascend
from havoc wreaked within,
to grow slow and nurture wildly,
and never, no never, to look away.

Dear Vita, Don't Delay

Take me out of this violent world,
and be with me in our violet world,

carry me today to the meadow
brook of violet wine, and lay

me, Vita, in the violet moss, take me
out of this steel trap, lay me on a bed

of violet grass, wrap me in your violet
arms, in your whispers like petals

and pine needles, tell the violet leaves
you're mine, tell the disbelieving

moles and rats, tell the stained glass
panels of light that flood us

with the violet rays in our violet
chapel, what the moles don't know,

come with me and become violet
tell the jealous crows above, that we

were made for a violet world,
away from violence against violets,

a world where the only violence is
the violent love of violets, a world

where we are tender violets
in the violets, and I'm your tender love,

loved violetly, O, Vita, come with me
and live where harps and hearts foray,

take me out of this violent world,
and be with me in our violet world.

For Truth Stated Plainly is in Danger

Our souls will not cower:
when there's no place
to send our secrets,
we'll hide them
where they can thrive
safely, beneath the ivy
armor of poetic obscurity,
for truth stated plainly
is in danger of mutiny
brought on by surveillance,
but truth veiled in art travels on.

Under a Sixfold Sun

She knows the intricacies
of you, the flora of frigidity
in you; these, she has studied
across ages, across rainbows,
and she knows the rays
that make them appear
in the overdo dew of you,
how to cast in you the rays
that melt the past and future
into a molecule, when you were
two ice crystals destined
to coalesce as one,
your solidarity, crystalline,
your origins, hexagonal,
your variant, unrecognizable;
a translucent nucleus of harpy
happenstance in the ice garden
under a sixfold sun.

Roots

I do not know if I have killed
desire, in the name of resistance,
or if I have sealed desire
in the restless but distilled
unconscious, where it accumulates
and waits to be punctured
and released into consciousness;
I hope for the latter, predict
the former, fill my mind
like a clock with demarcations,
divisions of the whole,
and I become the thing that keeps
going but cannot wonder
if time is ruin or if I am
waiting for the opening of an end;
inside this machine is a cog
that will prove prophetic,
inside this primality is a death
that will give way to tomorrow;
it is in this ghost of birthing
future that what I've killed
will be born, what I've stowed
will become the Ecstatic;
the softness of blossoms
disguise the eruption of life,
that flowers are explosives,
proving that not all detonation
is harm; I will be the thing
that opens to now but does not
release what is born — the seed
and the flower do not part:
there is no separation beyond
our illusion; the birth in me
belongs to you, and you are life
with roots in me,
my sole and soul's futurity.

Hanami on the First Day of Spring
(A Schoolyard Liturgy for the Winter-Buried)

Sit with me while the cherry blossoms blossom,
side by side on a petaled bench forgotten,

stay with me as the merry seasons fly,
and with your cherry side glances, make the cherry

skies sigh and the cherry fountains fountain,
with your soft kind hands pressed into my blossoms,

across the cherry pages of blossom bound
time, let your cherry thoughts blossom

and your blossoms unwind, as you stray, as you
sway across my cherry ribbon strands

and my white wilting thighs, watch my cherry kisses
fall and lift you like a cherry butterfly

into the cherry blossom clouds adrift, above
the cherry trees on high and through the cherry bands,

into the cherry blossom lands, through the cherry
blossom bog into the cherry blossom brambles

and through the cherry blossom fog
up to the pinnacle of cherry blossom heights, oh, lover-

not-forgotten, glide into these cherry blossom sights
with your cherry blossom sprite and float on rivers

of cherry blossom light into our cherry blossom
youth, pressed into petals of the past, lost

in the blossoms of our cherry petaled truth,
I beckon you to blossom, as the merry seasons fly,

I watch for you to blossom in the cherry blossom
skies, and for your heart to bloom and soften,

like your hands upon my thighs, and for your cherry
footsteps to fall on the path of endless blossoms

that you find, sit with me side by side on a petaled
bench of a thorny past forgotten,

while the cherry blossoms blossom.

And Now I Live for the Flowers

And now I live for the flowers,
the petals that wither, the petals
that quiver, the petals that wait

for the bedfellow mist, the drip
on the lip of the primrose's slip,
the petals that sip, a garden apart,

and now I live for the hour of art,
the heady violets and paw print
pinks, the strokes and the smoke

of the brambling ink, and now
I live for the kitchen sink, the sight
of green, the hosta in need, the host

of the bloodthirsty spiderlings,
the butter dish, my silent wish,
to be one with what's in my midst

yet still to be with what's beyond,
beyond my lawn, beyond my sky,
beyond the never tiring sighs,

and now I live for Sappho's lyre,
the you shaped harp of my desire,
the hand that plucks, the hand

that holds, my life devoted to her
odes, the gamut of the ancient
codes, the rose confounded by her

pose, gardens that shimmer,
the shawls on the shoulders of girls
who shiver with crisscross looks,

and now I live for the library books,
the decadent crannies, the plushy
nooks, the canvas bags hung

on the hooks, a den remote,
and now I live for stones that float,
for rivers aflow, for rivers that know,

for rushes that spread the petticoat
like a mossy moat, across my soul,
across the thoughts I have to stow,

across the decks and necks of fathers,
across the tender streams of water,
and now I live for my daughters.

How Grief and I Relate

When will you feel this grief,
when will you let me through,
my grief says to me, in slanted sighs,
never, I say to Grief, and then I rise
to set her apart and put her in a glass
vase of oddities I want to preserve,
that linger between pass(t) and tresspass(t),
and then I send her up into a cloud,
to watch her rumble, mournful in a shroud,
and then I release her to an ebullient
mass, a soft nether, a pillow of wet
divine relief, a sacred bruise,
and when she comes raining
my world gray, her saturation met,
she does so from that place, (s)wept
with sun and moon and starful grace:
this is how grief and I relate.

In This Reality, Rare

It was not what we expected, what happened there,
on the bench, together, snakes did not shoot
like tulips out of my head, nor did the sky rip in half,
nor did it flood us with a horizon the color of blood,
you did not dissolve into a disappearing bliss, nor
did you undulate like the water logged phoenix,
nor did the noir become the eclipse of the earth
by the command of the scepter from a hand above,

It was not what we expected, what happened then,
in that kiss, together, you did not flash like a bulb
unscrewed from the wired wall, between beast
and doll, you did not crumble into a dried up leaf,
nor did you spread yourself in the growing dew for
all to see, nor did you shush me while you brushed
me with the clematis and crumbling soil of your buried
alchemy, nor did my sobs interrupt us as we drowned.

It will not be what we expect, what happens now,
in this reality, the bugged walls and plugged ears
of fear won't crush our dreams, you will not deny
me, nor will you refuse to recognize me, nor will I have
to refract myself into sea glass fragments and piece
myself back into a semblance of a former me, and you
will not duck and cover when a holy child draws near,
the chariots of angels will not give you day terrors,

nor will deceit ruin us with its reign of error, nor will
we be anywhere except unbearably bare, past silver,
past gold, past opal and aqua, past young, past old,
nor will we be anywhere but everywhere, we will not
be as we are now, fixed into a nightmare, chained
into a nonsensical narrative, nor will we be writhing
with rage in the margins of convention, nor will we be
so ensnared in a time of deathtraps and suspensions,

nor will we be anything but on the bench, in that kiss,
in this reality, rare and without care: there, then, and now.

From Sky to You

The night is a reflection of a well-lit room,
candles at every corner, doubled,
and doubles of the in between objects
of selfhood, including the self, staring
back at itself, objectified, yet the room
and everything in it is infused
with all that the moon touches,
even in her hiding, we are all The Two
Fridas, floating, hand in hand,
breathing through an umbilical of glass,
witnessing self through the unseen and seen.
I enter the room, holding a candelabra
to see myself walk the night, midair,
across the lane, across the line of trees,
across the path hidden behind them,
across the yellow cross-gartered oak,
across my fingers with bows and strings,
across the drive, over the stop signs
and the signs stopped, to the other pane
that, with the sun and in the day,
brings me from sky to you.

Pansy Lips

I spread   my ether

above

and 'neath her,

I seal her
in

    my envelope;
               she opens

pansy lips that dote
and float
in hope
that

I will please her.

You Pair Well With Me

Elegance is another word for mercy,
or should be—
for there can be no elegance
without mercy. And there can be no
flavor without substance, no spice
without good intention, no cloves
without a foundation of flora.

You come to me with more than
a clinging hint—
of clove, more than the mystery of balsam,
when you come in for the mouthfeel,
you come to me on the firstpalate,
you come for me on the midpalate,
and you come with me on the finish.

I come to you, cedar-planked and pink,
a peach seared with sincerity, elegant,
I weep as the maples weep, when they weep
to bring sweetness to the lips of the bark,
to the animal in need, and it is mercy
that makes you pair well with me.

The Well of Lo

Awoke awash,
awash with grief,

ebbing and tiding
in care of calendric

[wine dark she]
up she stood me,

up to greet
the Lunar Lady

Mac-bed(b/ae/th)andbeyond
who fell

and said 'go slow'
'go flow'

and learn to t'read
the well of Lo

(-neliness)

You, Becoming a Flower in Bloom

I fear what I cannot hear:
the sounds of muted mornings
on side streets, the unapparent white
crimes, the diminished howls
under the fan swept air,
the future of desire,
the absence of a future at all.

I crave a moment with the truth:
the expression on your face
as you hold a box of my letters,
you, fingering the oceanic harp
of my heart, its melody inside you,
like butterflies twirling, you,
becoming a flower in bloom,
your warm laughter, the serpents
in your garden-dreams.

I love what I know:
life itself and its surprising kisses
on my unwashed hair and wounded
finger-tips, the you you were not
brave enough to realize,
the you I wait to embrace,
in this hourglass lifetime.

My Petals Weep

I lift you in a line,
delivering you the aria in me
that none but you can hear.

Your lids close as pads of lily
over your thoughts: I am as still
as a molten flower after a bath of fire.

In my greenhouse dreams,
with watercolor stains of blue peony,
it is you who lift me.

My lips open, slowly, unseen,
and your hot hues melt and seep,
a silent night: my petals weep.

Perennial

Some days, we are nursery
brimming with impatient annuals,
which come and then go,
palm plants in palm rooms,
but what is within us
does not ride on wagon wheels,
is not brought in as cargo:
for you are my perennial.

Some days, we are a church,
a history, raftered and echoing,
a throng of flames, cast
on porcelain veils and rosy
cheeks, towers of broken pieces
angled for the light, a prayer held
as tenderly as a buttercup
before the altar of a chin.

But it is Palm Sunday, when
our nursery is church, so I am
as ghostly and green as resin
air: the frankincense to your myrrh,
I hold your hand, fill your palms
with the flowers of my fingers,
and only you can feel me linger
for I am your perennial.

What's A Sunflower

Why is it not better understood
that a flower is always burning?

She takes hyrr life from a distant heat;
it moves in hymn, undoes the freeze.

Why is it not better understood
that you are always burning with me?

What is: the paradox of what is soft
and hard, a riddle, like the moon?

These Words, My Vespers

These words, my vespers
for you: for you have made my life
an unending vigil, a sweet
ceaseless solitude, a desperate plea,
a sorrowful ballad on a sullen harp.

These times don't know me,
these days, a barricade against truth,
yet I am in the tranquil night garden
of my longing, safe in the harbor
of my desire for you.

An errant fool dares to wrench me
from my yearning, to distract me
from my burning, to stake
the flowing gown of my fragrant
odes to the dirt, to build a fence.

Here, from aloft, I throw down
the twisted vines, a verdant litany
 of all I have suffered for you,
and bid you climb, gather my clematis
as you go, then hoist me home.

Is Grief a Demon or a Daffodil?

Across the street, a girl comes
to know the demon of grief.

Her body trembles for months,
her face shrivels, she shrinks.

But years later she blossoms,
once she's made it through

the gates of trembling, once
what shriveled her expands

her: a hellion? a trumpet of truth?

Jessica Lowell Mason teaches courses in writing, literature, history, and gender and sexuality studies at the University at Buffalo, Bard College with the Bard Prison Initiative, Buffalo State University, and Niagara University. She is a doctoral candidate at the University at Buffalo, and is a research assistant with the Center for Disability Studies and the Gender Institute as part of their Mellon Foundation-funded "Communities of Care" project. Her first book of poetry, *Straight Jacke*t, a finalist selected by Sarah Freligh for the Eugene Paul Nassar Poetry Prize, was published by Finishing Line Press in 2019. Selections of her writing have appeared in *The Gay and Lesbian Review, Sinister Wisdom, Lambda Literary, Gender Focus, The Comstock Review, Lavender Review, Wilde Magazine, The Feminist Wire, Mad in America, Humanities,* and *Praeger*. She is the co-editor of *Madwomen in Social Justice Literatures, Movements, and Art* (Vernon Press, 2023) and the co-founder of Madwomen in the Attic, a feminist mental health literacy organization in Buffalo, NY. She is a member of and workshop leader with the Mad Writing Collective.

www.ingramcontent.com/pod-product-compliance
Lightning Source LLC
Chambersburg PA
CBHW030055170426
43197CB00010B/1541